A Tribute to the People's Princess

A Tribute to the People's Princess

Peter Donnelly

Credits

For Quadrillion:
The editorial team: Will Steeds, Chris Stone, Bron Kowal, Phil de Ste. Croix, Jane Alexander
The design team: Sue Mims, Sarah Newby, Teddy Hartshorn
Nicky Chapman, Justina Leitão, Chris Dymond
Production: Gerald Hughes (Production Director), Ruth Arthur, Karen Staff
Colour reproduction: Square Precision Graphics, London

For Bookman Projects: Nick Kent, Hugh Gallacher

Author

PETER DONNELLY, born in County Durham, UK, in 1941, is a widely admired author, biographer and journalist. He has known and written about many famous figures, but has been most highly praised for his book *Mrs. Milburn's Diaries,* the moving story of an ordinary woman who lived through the war years in Coventry. Peter is responsible, along with Nigel Dempster, for the creation of the *Daily Mail Diary*.

Publisher's acknowledgements

The Publishers would particularly like to thank the following people for their help on this project: Nick Kent at Bookman Projects Ltd. for his advice and help throughout the project; James Whitaker of *The Mirror* for his unselfish assistance; Hugh Gallacher for specialist picture research; Alison Hynds for consultancy and picture editing; Jill Palmer, Gill Swain, Lucy Turner, Jan Disley, Ollie Picton-Jones for invaluable editorial contributions; Ric Papineau, of the Academy of Excellence, for his good offices; everyone in Mirror Group's IT department for their help and advice.

5089 A B C D E F

This edition first published in the United States in 1997 by Sweetwater Press.

Printed in the United States by RR Donnelley & Sons Co.

9 8 7 6 5 4 3 2 1
Digit on the right indicates the number of this printing
Library of Congress Cataloging-in-Publication Number 97-75322
ISBN 1-889372-81-1

This book was produced by CLB International, Godalming, Surrey, U.K.
in cooperation with Bookman Projects Ltd.

Published by Sweetwater Press, an imprint of
Running Press Book Publishers
125 South Twenty-second Street
Philadelphia, Pennsylvania 19103-4399

Contents

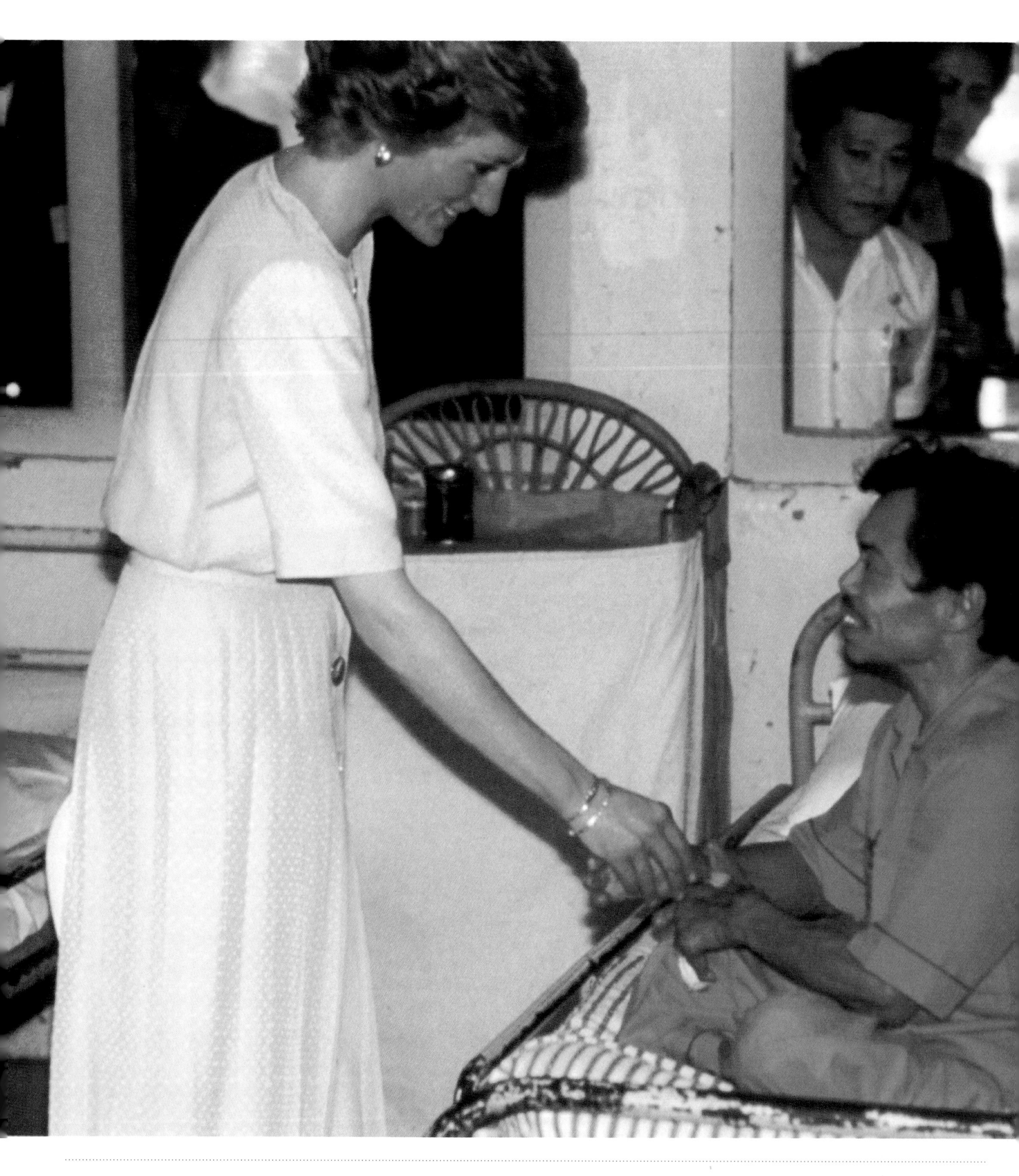

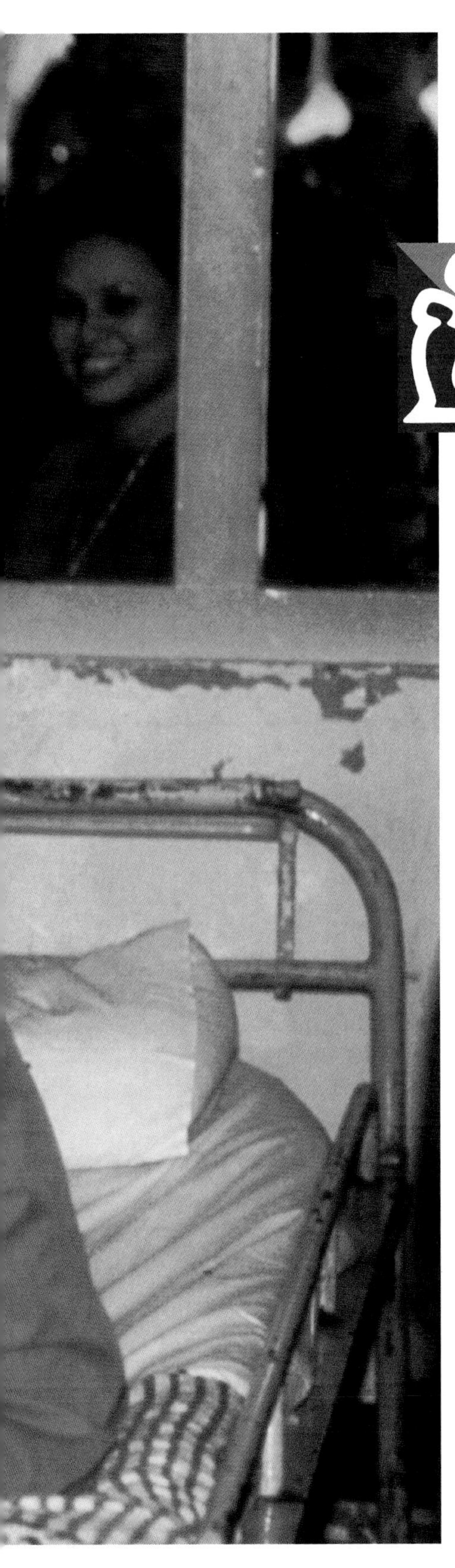

Foreword

I am delighted to have been asked to write the Foreword to *Diana: A Tribute to the People's Princess*. She became Patron of The Leprosy Mission in 1990, after visiting a leprosy hospital despite adverse advice and criticism. Leprosy may not only be mentally and physically damaging, but it is often erroneously seen as a curse from the gods, and the 'victims' then become outcasts. Since Diana herself was the frequent victim of pain and anguish, she had a special empathy for those who suffered in the same way. It is not a coincidence that five of her six remaining charities are associated with stigma.

She was charismatic, witty and, above all, a woman of extraordinary compassion. This was demonstrated both in the limelight and, more often, when there were no cameras or reporters present. On one occasion in Harare she was touring a hospital ward run by The Leprosy Mission when she saw a patient with badly deformed hands using a sewing machine to make a dress. She asked me about the lady sewing and a ward nurse replied, 'She came in a leper and is going out a person; a Christian seamstress'. Instead of proceeding along the ward as expected, the Princess disappeared behind a partition. She was in tears. It was not because she felt sorry for the lady, but rather she was so overwhelmed by the recovered hope and dignity which the lady now possessed.

She was a huge force for good, now gone from the world. Her power lay not in political status but in the wealth of her overwhelming compassion for those in need. I am grateful that this book will, in some way, help perpetuate her work and her memory.

Tony Lloyd

The Reverend Tony Lloyd,
Executive Director,
The Leprosy Mission,
Peterborough PE2 5GZ, UK

The Making of a Princess

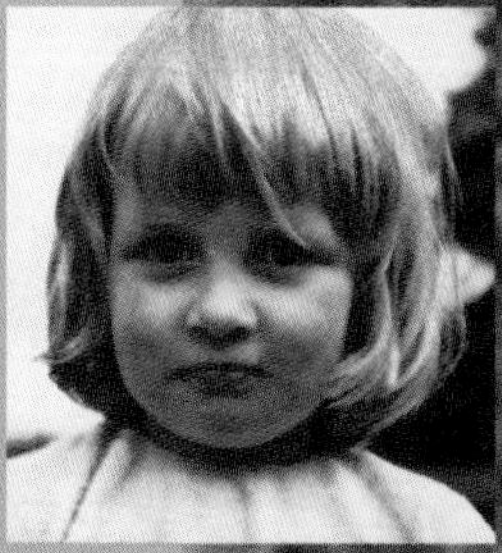

"Diana was very fond of pretty clothes and kept them neat. She loved floral dresses and used to go shopping with her mother for party outfits…She wasn't easy. Some children that young will do as they are told immediately, but Diana wouldn't, it was always a battle of wills. She was full of spirit. But she was a lovely child, and after she had been reasoned with she would usually co-operate – eventually."

Lessons in life for a young lady

She always knew she was set apart somehow, and once said as much, without sounding in the least pompous: 'I was always detached from everyone else. I knew I was going somewhere different, that I was in the wrong shell.'

That 'somewhere different' was a privileged place as an icon of her age, a woman instantly recognised in every corner of the globe, a glamorous but still very accessible cover-girl hailed as 'the People's Princess' and finally, through her compassion and concern for others and her absolute commitment to them, as the 'Queen of People's Hearts', a role she craved above all others.

There was an initial public misconception that Diana Spencer, the first Englishwoman to marry an heir to the throne for more than 300 years, was in fact 'just an ordinary girl'. Far from it: the Honourable Diana Frances Spencer was born at Park House, on the Queen's Sandringham estate in Norfolk, late in the afternoon of July 1, 1961.

She was the third daughter of Viscount Althorp, the eighth Earl Spencer, who had been an equerry both to George VI and the Queen. Her maternal grandmother, Ruth, Lady Fermoy, was a close friend and lady in waiting to the Queen Mother. And through these close links with the British royal family, she became a childhood playmate of her future husband's younger brothers, Prince Andrew and Prince Edward.

Hers, though, was a far from happy childhood. When she was just six years old, her mother left her father for the wallpaper heir Peter Shand Kydd, depriving Diana of the full-time mother-love that she came to believe was so vitally important for her own children, and others.

The Viscountess sought custody of her two youngest children, Diana and Charles Althorp,

Top: Park House, Sandringham, where Lady Diana Spencer was born on July 1, 1961. Above: Early years should be a time of joy for a family, but Diana's childhood was to be overshadowed by growing disharmony between her parents.

but was thwarted by her mother Ruth, who told the court they should remain with their father. The couple were divorced in 1969 and Diana continued to live at Park House until the death of her grandfather, the seventh Earl, in 1975.

The family then moved to the Spencer family seat at Althorp House in Northamptonshire, but this change of home did not signal a happier new stage in Diana's life. She would

"I shall only get married when I am sure that I am in love, so that we will never be divorced."

tiptoe downstairs and, leaning over the banisters, watch as her mother and father bitterly fought out their continuing battles.

But most of the time she hid her face in the bed covers. She developed a fear of the dark and had bad dreams: 'I just couldn't bear it. It was a testing time.'

For Diana, the day her mother packed her bags and left meant a succession of nannies, most of whom described her as 'difficult' or 'tricky'. She told one of them, Mary Clarke: 'I shall only get married when I am sure I am in love, so that we will never be divorced.'

Another nanny, Janet Thompson, who started work with Diana when she was just three years old, recalls: 'She would call out to me to bring her a glass of water or to take her to the loo in the middle of the night. Sometimes she would wake up after a bad dream and would cry. I would have to talk to her gently. Then in the morning she would come into my room and creep into bed with me to keep warm, and for a cuddle.'

Even at that age, Diana had a passion for two things which stayed with her all her life – clothes and sweets. Nanny Janet Thompson remembers:

Above: Diana the tomboy. In fact, even as a young child she was already very fond of pretty dresses and loved shopping for clothes with her mother.

'Diana was very fond of pretty clothes and kept them neat. She loved floral dresses and used to go shopping with her mother for party outfits.

They were a very sociable family, and were out all the time at tea parties, so Diana needed a good choice.' But sometimes her young charge could be a handful: 'She wasn't easy. Some children that young will do as they are told immediately, but Diana wouldn't, it was always a battle of wills. She was full of spirit. But she was a lovely child, and after she had been reasoned with she would usually co-operate – eventually.'

Though she played with the royal children when she was young, Diana never shared their enthusiasm for horses and dogs. Elder sister Sarah was horse mad, but Diana never saw the point of it all. Once, when she was 10, the sisters went riding together. Diana's horse bolted and she was thrown off, breaking her arm.

She was wary of horses from then on, although after her marriage she did try to please the Queen and Prince Philip by trying to learn to ride well, but gave it up as a bad job.

Nanny Thompson's departure coincided with the breakup of the marriage of Viscount Althorp and his wife, a traumatic time for their children. But it was nothing compared to the arrival of the new woman in their father's life – the formidable Raine Spencer, or 'Acid Raine' as they came to call her.

The children so hated Raine – the former Countess of Dartmouth and daughter of the romantic novelist Barbara Cartland – that they composed poison-pen letters to try to drive her away.

If life at home was insecure, Diana's arrival at Sifield School in nearby King's Lynn in 1968 did little to improve matters. She was not as clever as her younger brother and he nicknamed her 'Brian' after the dim-witted snail in the children's TV show *The Magic Roundabout*.

'I longed to be as good as him in the schoolroom,' she recalled. 'I wasn't any good at anything. I felt hopeless, a drop-out. Brain the size of a pea – that's what I've got. I'm as thick as a plank.'

Nor did she do much better at Riddlesworth Hall, the boarding school near Diss in Norfolk to which she was sent when she was nine. In fact Diana would never shine academically – a fact cynics cruelly noted in later years – but she had other qualities which more than adequately compensated for her scholarly deficiencies.

Away from her family, painfully shy and lonely, she felt instant compassion for others suffering the same plight: 'She was awfully

Above: Playtime – nanny Janet Thompson and Diana play Blind Man's Buff while mother Frances holds Charles in her arms. Below: Diana and her younger brother Charles pictured in 1968.

Above: Family portrait. Behind the happy facade, the marriage was under strain. Left: Family snapshot. Diana, a rather round-faced three-year-old, poses for the camera.

sweet with the little ones,' her former head-teacher recalled. 'She could often be found comforting a tearful child, even though she was little more than a child herself.' Baby brother Charles, now Earl Spencer, also received the Diana mothering treatment.

In time Diana followed family tradition – and her mother and sisters Jane and Sarah – to West Heath, the all-girls public school near Sevenoaks in Kent, where, unsurprisingly to those who knew her, one of the most expensive educations that money can buy failed to help her win a single successful examination result. She failed all her 'O' levels, even at the second taking, and left the school at 16.

But she had done well at sport, especially swimming, netball and tennis, and she started ballet and tap-dancing lessons, which provided a welcome escape: 'It always released the tremendous tension in my head.'

And as West Heath encouraged pupils to visit the old and the sick, Diana found her forte. She spent hours visiting an old lady in a near-

Above: Diana, aged 11, at Sandringham with her pet guinea pig 'Peanuts'. From an early age she revealed an instinctive sympathy with people and animals.

Above: London, 1968. Diana's parents' marriage had broken down during the previous year.

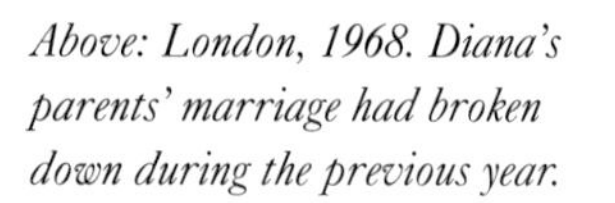

Above (and inset): By her own admission, Diana was not a star at school. 'Brain the size of a pea' was her candid self-assessment. Here she is seen at Riddlesworth Hall boarding school, where she started in 1970.

Above: On the Isle of Uist, a teenage Diana looks somewhat ill at ease in her country casuals
Right: A carefree moment with Shetland pony 'Soufflé' in the summer of 1974 at her mother's estate in Scotland.

by town – and while others were unwilling to visit the local mental hospital, Diana found an instant rapport with the handicapped teenagers.

After a brief stay at the Institut Alpin Videmanette, an expensive Swiss finishing school, her father bought her a small flat in Coleherne Court on the borders of London's Kensington – and the 19-year-old Diana embarked upon what – in later days – she would look back on as one of the happiest periods of her life.

Sharing the flat with three best girlfriends, she was at last free to do as she pleased. On three days a week, she worked for well-heeled friends, cleaning floors for £1 an hour, serving canapes at cocktail parties and acting as nanny. Then she took a job for which she was ideally suited, as an assistant working with young children at the Young England kindergarten in Pimlico.

Very soon now she would become public property – her life would never be the same again for the eyes of the world were to be turned upon her. But for now she spent happy, giggling days with her friends, enjoying life to the full.

Left: Even as a young teenager, Diana displayed a natural poise in front of the camera, tempered by a hint of diffidence. This girl would become one of the most photographed women in the world.

The girl who clicked with the camera

It wasn't long before the young Diana was spotted by one of Britain's most experienced royal-watchers – James Whitaker of *The Mirror*. He recalls 'I first set eyes on her in January, 1978. I was captivated'.

Whitaker noticed the attractive 16-year-old standing next to Prince Charles while he was out shooting pheasants with seven other guns at Sandringham:

'She was peering at me and a photographer colleague down a long, tree-lined path through a pair of powerful binoculars', he says. 'But as they were still attached by a strap to Charles' neck, his head was at a funny angle!'

'They were both laughing uproariously, and very clearly happy. But I was mystified why it was Diana standing with Charles and not her sister, Lady Sarah, who was his girlfriend at the time and was also at Sandringham. My immediate thought was that she was there "for Prince Andrew".'

But by July 1980, just a few months before the 'Romance of the Century' began, Diana was spotted again and again wherever Charles happened to be – at a polo match at Cowdray Park in West Sussex, and at the Braemar Gathering, the highlight of the Highland Games season.

After the Gathering, Diana caught the afternoon flight back to London with two men who would figure largely in her life – Nicholas Soames, an Equerry to Charles (and a Minister in Britain's

Above: Diana's romance with Prince Charles catapaulted her into the headlines.

Above: Just a few weeks before the announcement of her engagement in 1981, Diana is seen with her colleagues at the Young England kindergarten in Pimlico. Below: Outside her Kensington flat.

Above: Diana was proud to be a bridesmaid at the wedding of her sister Lady Jane to Robert Fellowes at the Guard's Chapel in London in April 1978.

Conservative Government) and Colonel Andrew Parker Bowles, the husband of Camilla – who later loomed large in Diana's life.

For a short while, Diana's life in London continued as normal. Every morning she and her flatmates – Ann Bolton, Carolyn Pride and Virginia Pitman – took turns going for the morning newspapers and milk for breakfast. But not for long. The Press were on to Charles' girl – this 'Lady Di', as they dubbed her – and tracked her down to Coleherne Court, where battalions of reporters and cameramen pitched camp around the clock. From then on, the lenses hardly ever left her.

Among the best-known pictures of the Princess taken at the time was of her at the kindergarten where she worked, with one child balanced on her hip and the sunlight shining through her dress. 'Diaphanous Di' looked stunning, shy, beguiling, and a popular myth is that photographers 'set her up' for this picture.

Not true, according to those who were there. She was simply walking by some bushes, and the photographers took their pictures. Only later, when the film was developed, did they realise her legs could be seen so well.

Above: Diana and Camilla Parker Bowles – companionship was to turn to rivalry.

Above: The famous picture of 'Diaphanous Di' was taken at the Young England kindergarten in 1980. Reportedly its publication made Diana cry.

Diana falls in love with the man who will be King

As the weeks went on, Diana continued to enchant and enthral all who met her, and huge pressure was being put on Prince Charles to do something about the delightful girl who many believed to be the perfect mate for him.

Of her first meeting with Charles, Diana remembered: 'He was just somebody who was always around. I don't remember a great deal about it. But I do know that it was when I was still wearing nappies. It's funny, but the best things happened to me when I was still in nappies!'

Above: Preparations for the wedding occupied the spring months of 1981. Here Diana and Prince Charles are seen on the steps of St Paul's Cathedral in London.

But her first proper meeting with the Prince came much later, when she was a gawky 16-year-old and he was courting her sister Sarah. 'I remember being podgy, no make-up, an unsmart lady', she said. 'But I made a lot of noise and he seemed to like that.'

Another meeting came when she was invited to stay with friends at Petworth, in West Sussex, in July, 1980. She sat next to Charles on a hay bale and commiserated with him over the death of Earl Mountbatten. 'You looked so sad when you walked up the aisle at the funeral,' she told him. 'It was the most tragic thing I've ever seen. My heart bled for you when I watched it. I thought "It's wrong. You are lonely. You should be with somebody to look after you".'

A series of dates followed, and by December that year there were rumours that an engagement announcement was imminent. James Whitaker talked to Diana for a long time about the situation: 'She would not commit herself to anything', he recalls, 'But she assured me that marrying into the Royal Family would not be a problem for her. She made it clear that as she was literally brought up next door to Sandringham House, she was used to the Royal Family.'

Even so, the new pressure on her was enormous. Her phone never stopped ringing and she was followed everywhere by photographers. In public she bore the attention bravely. She told the pressmen: 'I like to think I get on very well with most of you. The only thing that really annoys me is when my children (at the kindergarten) get frightened by things like flashguns.'

Behind the scenes, though, the constant pressure was taking its toll, even in those early days: 'I cried like a baby to the four walls,' she confessed. 'I just couldn't cope with it.'

On February 6, 1981 Charles formally proposed to Diana at Windsor Castle, and that night she plonked herself down on her bed and asked her flatmates: 'Guess what?'

'He asked you?', they yelled. 'He did', she laughed, 'and I said "Yes, please!" I never had any doubts about it.' Soon afterwards she moved forever from Coleherne Court, begging her flatmates to keep in touch. 'I'll need you more than ever now', she said, as she headed off to Clarence House, official London home of the Queen Mother, where she was to stay until the marriage.

> *"I remember being podgy...an unsmart lady. But I made a lot of noise and he seemed to like that."*

The engagement was announced three weeks later and the happy couple appeared together on TV, with Diana proudly showing off her engagement ring and her enchanting shyness. 'Are you in love?' the interviewer asked. 'Of course', Diana replied. 'Whatever love is', added the Prince wryly.

Later, it was said that Diana had reservations about the match, even up to the eleventh hour – and that she had to be persuaded to go ahead with it by her sisters, with their half-joking jests that the souvenir tea-towels were already on sale.

But if there were doubts about the wisdom of a match between a shy nursery school assistant and a settled bachelor who had been raised to become king, no-one voiced them at the time.

Above: The happy couple posed for photographers on the garden steps at Buckingham Palace after the official announcement of their engagement was made on February 24, 1981. Charles had proposed to Diana at Windsor Castle less than three weeks earlier.

Far left: The official engagement picture was taken by Lord Snowdon. Diana's ring featured a large sapphire surrounded by glittering diamonds.

This page (clockwise from above): Charles and Diana take a break at Balmoral before the wedding; seen together in informal mood returning to the Prince's car; at their first public engagement together – a gala charity concert in aid of the Royal Opera House held at Goldsmith's Hall in London; and Diana embracing the Duke of Kent at the Wimbledon Lawn Tennis Championships in 1981, shortly before her wedding day.

Above: On the second day of Royal Ascot, June 17, 1981, Diana appeared with the Queen and the Queen Mother wearing a delicate peach skirt and top. By now, all eyes were on her.

"Are you in love?"
"Of course." Diana replied.
"Whatever love is," added the Prince wryly.

Right: Diana and Princess Anne at a polo match at Windsor Great Park. As a result of an accident in childhood, Diana did not much enjoy the sport of riding.
Below: As Diana began to find her feet in the public eye, her sense of poise and self-assurance blossomed.

The Fairytale that Faded so Soon

"I always had my doubts about how he really felt. There was never anything concrete for me to grab a hold of, but I did have these feelings about things, that things weren't quite right…One minute I was a nobody. The next minute I was Princess of Wales…it was just too much for one person to handle."

Joy for the world – and the 'luckiest girl'

Fairytale. It's an easy, glitzy word, not least for headline writers. But this time, strangely, it seemed to fit the scenario perfectly: the bachelor prince, after a string of well-publicised romances, had at last found his true love, and she was beautiful and beguiling and becomingly shy and they'd live happily ever after.

Except, of course, as we now know, that even as they talked of love on television, the Prince was having a relationship with Camilla Parker Bowles, an old girlfriend who had married someone else.

Despite that the wedding ('of the century', as some inevitably described it) at St Paul's Cathedral on July 29, 1981, was a model of the pomp and pageantry at which the British excel. They nervously muddled each other's names. Even the Archbishop of Canterbury said it was 'the stuff of fairy tales'. And that long, lingering kiss on the Buckingham Palace balcony made front pages in newspapers and magazines around the globe.

"I thought I was the luckiest girl in the world when I looked at Charles through my veil. I had tremendous hope in my heart."

Diana remembered that before the wedding there had been her first official engagement – a London charity gala. 'It was a horrendous occasion', she said. 'I hadn't a clue what I was meant to be doing. I know people think all sorts of people gave me lessons…but they didn't. Nobody helped me at all.'

One person she met that night sympathised: Princess Grace of Monaco laughed and told Diana: 'Don't worry – it will get a lot worse'. They posed with Charles for pictures – Grace looking every inch Her Serene Highness, and Diana appearing shy and nervous in the presence of the former Hollywood film star who'd swapped her role as Grace Kelly to become a fairytale princess when she married Prince Rainier of Monaco.

Their lives, Diana could not help but reflect, were running on remarkably similar courses – and she shared the world's shock and sadness when, in the September of the following year, Princess Grace was killed in a horrifying car crash, leaving her husband

Above: A proud father escorts his daughter up the aisle at St Paul's Cathedral.

Above: Amid all the excitement of her wedding day, Princess Diana finds a moment to talk to her bridesmaids on their return to Buckingham Palace after the church ceremony.

Above: The fairytale wedding: Diana travelled from Clarence House to St Paul's in the Glass Coach, a suitably romantic conveyance for such a leading lady.

and young family to grieve for an attractive and much-loved woman who had done so much, and on an international scale, to help others less fortunate than herself.

As her wedding day approached, Diana became increasingly nervous: 'In 12 days' time I shall no longer be me', she told her dance teacher. And on the day itself she woke early for what she later described as 'the most emotionally confusing day of my life'.

She said: 'I thought I was the luckiest girl in the world when I looked at Charles through my veil. I had tremendous hope in my heart. At the age of 19 you always think you're prepared for everything, and you think you know what's coming.

'No-one sat me down with a piece of paper and said "This is what's expected of you." But although I was daunted by the prospect at the time, I felt I had the support of my husband-to-be.'

Left: Diana and her Prince leaving the Cathedral. The wedding dress, designed by the Emanuels, was the talk of the moment.

Diana believed she had found her fairytale prince – and when she walked down the aisle, the world believed it, too. Swathed in oceans of ivory silk taffetta and with diamonds sparkling in her hair, she looked the perfect partner for Charles, resplendent in his Royal Navy uniform.

And their lavish wedding – in a year which had seen unprecedented violence in the inner cities of Britain – brought joy throughout the realm and to millions more around the world.

The newlyweds spent the first three days of their honeymoon at Broadlands, the peaceful Hampshire home of the Mountbatten family. But Diana's hopes of an idyllic romantic few days away from the media spotlight had already been dashed when her husband packed his fishing rods and half a dozen books.

This page: The newly married couple's return journey to Buckingham Palace through the streets of London was met with an outpouring of public acclaim and affection. The humanity and tenderness of the new Princess shone through all the pomp and circumstance and the pageantry.

Right: A radiant Princess Diana – all nervousness has been dispelled and her expression is one of sheer happiness.

After Broadlands they set off for a cruise of the Mediterranean aboard the royal yacht *Britannia*, which should have reinforced the commitment of a couple who had come to marriage in need of love and warmth and affection. But from the start it was clear that there would be massive problems to overcome.

Diana was determined to make it work: 'I think like any marriage, especially when you've had divorced parents like mine, you want to try even harder to make it work', she said. 'And you don't want to fall back into a pattern that you've seen happen in your own family.

'I desperately wanted it to work. I desperately loved my husband and I wanted to share everything together, and I thought that we were a very good team.'

But even on the honeymoon the cracks were starting to appear in the marriage as the presence of Camilla Parker Bowles in Charles' life became all too clear to Diana. She broke down and wept one day when two photographs of Camilla fell out of her new husband's diary.

Diana begged him to tell her the truth about his relationship with Camilla and how he felt about his new wife. But her pleas were ignored, and Charles gave no explanation, leaving her desperately unhappy, unsure and confused.

Even worse was the painful evening during the honeymoon when the couple entertained Egyptian President Anwar Sadat and his wife Jihan – and Charles arrived for dinner wearing a new pair of cufflinks in the shape of two interwoven Cs.

He said the gift from Camilla was merely a token of her friendship and nothing for his new bride to worry about. But Diana told friends later: 'I could not see why Charles needed these constant reminders of Camilla'.

After the honeymoon cruise, the couple returned to join the rest of the royal family for their traditional annual holiday on the Balmoral estate from August until October – and Diana hoped against hope that the media attention in her would now wane, if only a little.

Above and below: The famous kiss on the balcony of Buckingham Palace – a moment of spontaneity amid all the protocol and pageantry.

Above: Lord Lichfield's photograph of the Prince and Princess surrounded by their young bridesmaids and pages, and with best man Prince Andrew and Prince Edward, has a slightly informal feel that captures the joy of a young couple in love.

Right: The royal couple about to board an aircraft on the way to Gibraltar where they joined the royal yacht Britannia *for their honeymoon cruise in the Mediterranean.*

'When we were married they said that it would go quiet', she said. 'It didn't. And then it started to focus very much on me, and seemed to be on the front page of a newspaper every single day, which is an isolating experience.

'It took a long time to understand why people were so interested in me, but I assumed it was because my husband had done a lot of wonderful work leading up to our marriage. But then during the years you see yourself as a good product that sits on a shelf and sells well, and people make a lot of money out of you.'

She added: 'I was very daunted, because as far as I was concerned I was a fat, chubby, 20-year-old, and I couldn't understand the level of interest.'

> *"One minute I was a nobody. The next minute I was Princess of Wales, mother, media toy, member of this family."*

While at Balmoral the rows over Camilla continued. In public, they smiled for the cameras and Diana said she 'highly recommended married life'. But inside she was struggling with the knowledge that her husband was in love with someone else.

How did she cope? Much later she would say: 'I've got what my mother has got. However bloody you are feeling, you can put on the most amazing show of happiness. My mother is an expert at that and I've picked it up. It kept the wolves from the door'.

And of Charles, she said: 'I always had my doubts about how he really felt. There was never anything concrete for me to grab a hold of, but I did have these feelings about things, that things weren't quite right.'

Camilla was not the only problem in the marriage, though. Not least of the others was the 12-year age gap. She was a 20-year-old, young for her years, and he a 32-year-old who already seemed middle-aged. They had different characters, different desires, different enthusiasms. His older, wiser, friends intimidated and bored her. Her younger, brighter, set irritated him.

She did not much care for his polo or his country pursuits, which were the centre of his family's life. He was far from at home in discos or on the dance floor. And the differences soon put a great strain on the royal marriage.

Above and below: The honeymoon ends – a relaxed couple at Balmoral, August 1981.

Above: Aboard Britannia. *Charles and Diana spent 12 days cruising in the Mediterranean. Outwardly all seemed amicable, but already Charles' friendship with Camilla Parker Bowles was casting a shadow.*

Diana, abruptly removed from those happy, giggling, girlish days at the Coleherne Court flat to the strict conformity of court life, told her old friends she felt bewildered and lost. The building was remote, the courtiers unapproachable, the way of life stuffy and staid beyond belief. Even the intensive royal round of official home and foreign visits brought their own particular problem.

The huge crowds, Charles very soon came to realise, were turning out to see his glamorous new wife rather than him. Her presence electrified crowds and left him feeling left out of it: 'I might just as well stay in the car', he grumbled. But the crowds were creating problems for Diana, too.

The shy teenager quickly became a woman of violent mood swings, according to Charles' biographer, Jonathan Dimbleby. And often she would be in tears, saying she simply could not cope, as they travelled on to yet another royal appointment.

Diana became the 'Prisoner of Wales', trapped and frightened in an alien environment, and began to suffer from the slimmer's disease bulimia nervosa, characterised by bouts of binge eating and purging, which drove her to attempt to take her own life on more than one occasion.

Desperately trying to fit into the family

Above: Diana's first child, William, was born on June 21, 1982 at St Mary's Hospital, Paddington.

Soon after their honeymoon, as the couple posed for pictures on the banks of the River Dee, Di looked as thin as she had been in the weeks leading up to the wedding. But no-one was concerned. It was, after all, a demanding time for the girl.

And she was trying, desperately, to fit in. On their first official tour together, in the Principality of Wales, it never stopped raining and everyone was soaked. But Diana refused to wear an overcoat or mac, insisting that the public wanted to see her.

She was an instant smash hit by just being herself – no-one in the royal family had taught her anything, she said – and the crowd loved her for it. She was great at small talk and with the young kids and older people, and she never once complained about the appalling weather except in a jokey fashion. Diana-mania had begun.

But behind the scenes, a different picture of a deeply troubled Princess was emerging. Author Andrew Morton later claimed she slashed at her wrists with a razor blade, a penknife and a lemon slicer and once threw herself against a glass cabinet.

In January 1981, six months into the marriage and pregnant with William, she threw herself down the stairs at Sandringham. The Queen Mother was the first to arrive at the scene and was very shaken at what had happened. But Diana was lucky: she suffered severe bruising to her stomach, but she – and the baby she was carrying – were otherwise unharmed.

It was, she explained later, a cry for help: 'When no-one listens to you, or you feel no-one's listening to you, all sorts of things start to happen. For instance, you have so much pain inside yourself that you try and hurt yourself on the outside because you want help, but it's the wrong help you're asking for.

'People see it as crying wolf or attention-seeking, and they think because you're in the media all the time you've got enough attention...but I was actually crying out because I wanted to get better in order to go forward and continue my duty and my role as wife, mother, Princess of Wales. So yes,

I did inflict harm upon myself. I didn't like myself, I was ashamed because I couldn't cope with the pressures.'

During the next few weeks, before William was born in June, Diana suffered badly. She did not have a happy pregnancy, suffering from morning sickness, but continued with her public engagements and enchanted everyone she met.

It was a very frail-looking Diana who appeared on the steps of the hospital with William in her arms. And Charles appeared distant. Asked about married life, he said: 'It's all right, but it interferes with my hunting'.

Diana said of the birth: 'I felt the whole country was in labour with me. I felt enormous relief. But I had actually known William was going to be a boy, because the scan had shown it. So it caused no surprise.'

She added: 'When William arrived it was a great relief because it was all peaceful again, and I was well for a time'. But motherhood brought new pressures: 'One minute I was a nobody. The next minute I was Princess of Wales, mother, media toy, member of this family and...it was just too much for one person to handle.

Left and above: Four generations of a Royal Family on the occasion of William's christening, and the Queen Mother's birthday, on August 4, 1982.

Far left: Visiting Ayer's Rock on March 21, 1983 during the Royal Tour of Australia.
Left: Whenever she went walkabout, Diana was very much the star attraction, evidently somewhat to Prince Charles' chagrin.
Below: At the opening of the St John Ambulance Regional Centre in Alice Springs.

'Then I was unwell with post-natal depression, which no-one ever discusses. You have to read about it afterwards, and that in itself was a bit of a difficult time. You'd wake up in the morning and you didn't want to get out of bed. You felt misunderstood and just very, very low in yourself.

'I never had a depression in my life. But then when I analysed it I could see that the changes I'd made in the last year had all caught up with me, and my body had said "We want a rest".

'I received a great deal of treatment, but I knew in myself that actually what I needed was space and time to adapt to all the different roles that had come my way. I knew I could do it, but I needed people to be patient and give me the space to do it.

'It was a very short space of time. In the space of a year my whole life had changed, been turned upside down, and it had its wonderful moments. And I could see where the rough edges needed to be smoothed.'

Diana understood how her depression might have been daunting for the royal family: 'Maybe I was the first person ever to be in the family who ever had a depression or was ever openly tearful. And obviously that was daunting, because if you've never seen it before, how do you support it?'

Nothing, though, must interfere with royal duties, and in early 1983 Diana's duty was

Above: Just over two years after the birth of William, on September 15, 1984 Prince Harry was born. Here Charles and Diana leave St Mary's Hospital with him.

Above: Diana and Charles hold the month-old baby William. It is revealing to compare Diana's appearance in this photograph with the sophisticated woman carrying Harry (above left).

to tour Australia and New Zealand with her husband. The Royal Family wanted her to go without William. But she would not think of it. If she went, her new child had to go, too.

Buckingham Palace did not like the idea, but it worked. After landing in Australia, Diana installed William with nanny Barbara Barnes at a house in New South Wales and travelled there with Charles whenever they had a spare moment. In between, she carried out all her engagements and was a triumph wherever she went.

For Charles, though, it emphasised his second-billing status in public affection whenever he appeared with his wife. Crowds lining both sides of the street would groan when Charles was on their side. 'You've got me', he'd tell them, 'You'd better ask for your money back.' But he felt surplus to requirements and he didn't like it.

Nor did the Princess's progress from popular idol to semi-saint, achieved through her remarkable personal warmth as comforter of the sick, the dying and the needy, come easy for her husband. But she won worldwide acclaim for her espousal of the cause of AIDS victims, doing much to dispel the common belief that social contacts, such as shaking hands, could spread the disease.

And the British Government, realising that she was a major asset to the nation, could

Above: From Australia, the royal tour moved on to New Zealand. On April 23, William and his parents faced the cameras on the lawn of Government House in Auckland.

Above: The White House meets Saturday Night Fever – during the royal visit to America in 1985 Diana danced with John Travolta at a Washington gala. 'I'll give her ten out of ten', he enthused.
Right: Dancing the night away, Charles and Diana take to the floor.
Far Right: As a child Diana dreamed of becoming a ballerina. Here she appears on stage with Wayne Sleep for charity in 1985.

Above: Diana exhibits her wicked sense of fun, and Charles seems to be enjoying the joke.
Below: At the Live Aid concert in 1985. Diana greatly enjoyed rock music and live concerts.

Top: Diana and Pope Paul II, 1985.
Above: A public display of affection at a Windsor polo match in 1983.

not wait to get her into a country to help boost goodwill and exports. The tours came in quick succession: to Spain, to France, a magnificent two-week visit to Italy, to Portugal, to America and later to Brazil, Japan and India.

But within the Royal Family, the Princess seems to have been regarded as an uncontrollable 'wild card' and to have been isolated accordingly. No single event can be said to have caused the breakdown of the marriage. The Prince told TV viewers that he was faithful to Diana until the relationship had 'irretrievably broken down' in the second half of the 80s.

The Princess's estimate of when the marriage died is earlier. She says it was effectively over after the birth of her second son, Prince Harry, in September 1984. Charles had hoped for a girl, and a dismissive remark – 'Oh it's a boy and he's even got rusty hair' – marked the beginning of the end. 'From that moment, something inside me died', the Princess told friends.

Rage and rows were reported as commonplace. The Prince stuck rigidly to his annual schedule of polo, hunting, shooting and fishing, regardless of school holidays or family weekends. The Princess sank into the trough of bulimia.

Charles, taught from birth to keep his feelings under a tight rein and to himself, hid his unhappiness behind the mask of his royal duty. But his wife – more emotional, more theatrical, too highly strung and less well trained – was unable to camouflage her distress.

She grew to loathe the dinner parties Charles gave at Kensington Palace. She had little in common with many of the guests, was no gourmet and didn't particularly like wine – except in bursts, when she would binge on certain drinks.

Eventually she began going to bed before the party broke up, and after a year or two of trying her best – which wasn't good enough

– she started missing the dinner parties altogether. She acquired a young set of friends, more her own age, to spend time with. People like James Gilbey, a motor racing man with whom she had the famous 'Squidgy' telephone conversation, and Guards officers like Major David Waterhouse. She led a lonely existence. Occasionally she would go to the cinema at High Street Kensington, but often she would curl up at home with a book and get to bed early.

It seemed that the whole world was in love with Diana except her husband, and as a substitute for this lonely existence, she took on more and more engagements on behalf of her many charities – and worked out even harder in various gyms.

People who criticised her for going out to gyms and running the gauntlet of the dreaded paparazzi each morning didn't understand her need to get out from Kensington Palace. She felt cooped up there, incredibly frustrated.

'She has this great urge to go out and meet real people', an aide explained. 'Of course she could have a private gym at the palace, but she finds the place a little bit like prison.'

At the same time, Diana's relationship with her family was proving very difficult. Originally she got on very well with her mother, but in recent years that relationship had deteriorated. And in the last few months she was quite hostile about Frances Shand Kydd.

She was furious when Mrs Shand Kydd gave an interview in which she expressed the opinion that Diana was upset about the HRH tag being removed during her divorce settlement. At the same time, Diana's relationships with her brother Charles and sisters Sarah and Jane were up and down.

"She has this great urge to go out and meet real people. Of course she could have a private gym at the palace, but she finds the place a bit like a prison."

Volatile redhead Lady Sarah was once lady-in-waiting for Diana, but they didn't always get on that well. There was ever-present sibling rivalry – and always a bit of a problem that Sarah had been the girlfriend of Charles before Diana.

With brother Charles, Diana was unhappy when she was refused permission to create a home at the family seat, Althorp – and equally distraught at the breakdown of Charles' marriage to Victoria, and their subsequent departure for South Africa.

Top and above: By the mid-80s the strains in the marriage were taking their toll. However, in public photocalls, particularly with the children, appearances were maintained.

Above: Prince William's first day at his nursery school – an anxious occasion for pupil and mother alike.

Left and above: Diana relaxes with William and Harry during a summer holiday in Majorca in 1987. As a member of the Royal Family with a daunting schedule of appearances to undergo month after month, Diana cherished the time that she could spend in private with her sons, free from the pressures of public engagements, if not from the attentions of press photographers.

Seeking solace in the company of others

With Jane there was a problem, too. She is the easiest-going of all the Spencer children, but she is married to Sir Robert Fellowes, who is totally supportive of the Queen and took the royal side when it came to the divorce.

During the mid 80s, when the Prince and Princess were taking William and Harry on bucket-and-spade holidays to Majorca as guests of King Juan Carlos and the Queen of Spain, there was little physical or mental rapport between the two of them. And it was the events witnessed during a sunshine holiday in the summer of 1986 which first publicly exposed the growing cracks in the marriage.

"Are Charles and Di still in tune?" Buckingham Palace insisted everything was fine. But friends have said that after this trip to Majorca, the couple never slept together again.

Out for a day's cruise off Palma, Majorca, they did not exchange a single word with one another for the seven hours they spent on King Juan Carlos' motor yacht, the *Fortuna*. When Charles came up on deck Diana went below, and vice versa. Diana swam alone, Charles wind-surfed all by himself.

He came home three days early from Majorca, leaving behind his wife and sons, then aged four and two, and it was said that he was going fishing. But many later believed the real reason was that he wanted to join Camilla Parker Bowles in Scotland.

Newspapers asked, 'Are Charles and Di still in tune?' Buckingham Palace insisted everything was fine. But friends have said that after this trip to Majorca, the couple never slept together again.

Her husband's early departure set a pattern that was to become familiar over the next six years. They spoke little and appeared to go out of their way to avoid each other's company. At a polo match, Charles kissed his wife after losing a game. She scornfully wiped her lips with the back of her hand. Then, said witnesses, there was an extraordinary scene in the car park, where Diana appeared to kick out at her husband and he shoved her back against her car.

Elsewhere, all was going well enough. Diana was involved in numerous charities as Patron or President, and was a triumph, helping to raise millions of pounds for the organisations she was spearheading. And she was tireless in helping the disadvantaged and the poor.

When she attended an engagement she would always overrun her allotted time. Each child got a pat on the head, each mother or father kind words. She was faultless.

But Diana also began to feed on the adulation and adoration that the public gave her, and in some ways she no longer needed Prince Charles. By the end of the 80s he was no longer there for her.

Not for one moment, many believe, did Charles contemplate divorce, but emotionally he was involved with only one woman – Camilla Parker Bowles. And by now Diana had taken her own lover, James Hewitt.

The good-looking ex-cavalry officer had helped teach William and Harry to ride – and at the same time won the Princess' broken heart. In her infamous *Panorama* interview, Diana talked of how much she had 'adored' Hewitt in a relationship said to have lasted from 1986 until 1991. She also sought friendship with used-car dealer James Gilbey.

Above: Diana clowns with the Duchess of York on the ski slopes.
Right: Sarah Ferguson was another royal bride who challenged Palace orthodoxy.

The Prince continued to see Camilla – by ironic coincidence the great-granddaughter of Alice Keppel, mistress of Charles' great-great grandfather, Edward VII. And no-one seemed surprised when in 1988 author Anthony Holden published a biography portraying the royal relationship as a marriage of convenience.

Throughout 1988, the Princess was treated by eminent London psychiatrist Dr Maurice Lipsedge, sometimes for days at a time. He broke her dependency on the gorging and

This page (clockwise from top): The family on holiday in the Scilly Isles; Prince Harry's first day at Wetherby School; Diana competing in the mother's race at Wetherby School in 1990.

Above: Diana and her sons came to love winter sports in the Alps. Here they are seen on a chair lift at Lech in Austria in 1992.

rejection of food, which is the foundation of bulimia.

Friends say he made her see that the illness was a result of inner depression and insecurity and that, once she conquered that, the physical illness could be dealt with. And it was.

But the marriage had become a tyrrany of togetherness and seemed beyond treatment. Had they been an ordinary couple, they would undoubtedly have divorced years earlier.

They were christened 'The Glums'. The Princess looked positively gloomy at her husband's side, yet relaxed and friendly on her own. Charles, in turn, appeared cold and uninterested in his wife.

By 1991 the marriage was teetering on the edge, with a former royal policeman revealing: "They never smile, laugh or do anything together. They seem to want as little contact as possible."

By 1991 the marriage was teetering on the edge, with former royal policeman Andrew Jacques revealing: 'They never smile, laugh or do anything together. They seem to want as little contact as possible.'

In February 1992 they made a trip to India, where the Prince and Princess were not only in separate bedrooms but on separate floors of their palace. And the signs of open hostility between them were becoming more and more apparent.

On one truly grim day the couple split, with Charles staying behind in Delhi to address businessmen while Diana went off to Agra to visit Shah Jahan's magnificent Taj Mahal, the world's most romantic monument to love.

Diana made a huge point while at this mausoleum. She posed all alone in front of the edifice and looked downcast and forlorn. And Charles was left explaining that he'd not made a wise decision staying behind in the capital.

Too true. And a few days later, on the eve of St Valentine's Day, Diana made her biggest point ever when she turned her head away at the end of a polo match in Jaipur when Charles went to kiss her. He ended up brushing her ear, totally humiliated.

Above and top: As the marriage crumbled, Diana devoted more and more of her efforts to charity work. Her rapport with children was obvious in her visit to a deprived area in Brazil in 1991.

Top: Meeting the world famous tenor Luciano Pavarotti after his open-air concert in Hyde Park. Above: Two ladies of mercy meet in Rome in February 1992. Mother Teresa died just five days after Diana, on September 5, 1997.

In March 1992 Diana received devastating news – of the death of her much-loved father – while she was skiing in Lech, Austria, and Charles offered to fly back to Britain with her. She told him: 'It's a bit late to start acting the caring husband'.

But the Queen demanded that Diana allow Charles to accompany her, and she relented. The couple travelled together to Kensington Palace – and Charles immediately took off for Highgrove, leaving Diana to mourn alone.

A friend said 'Charles only flew home with her for the sake of his public image. She felt that at a time when she was grieving the death of her father, she should be given the opportunity of behaving as she wanted, rather than go through this masquerade.'

The cracks in the marriage had split wide open, and joint visits were not as many as before, but there was one ghastly tour still to come – to Korea in November, when the frostiness between them was awful to behold. After a couple of days it was as if they were on separate tours of the same country.

> *"We struggled along, we did our engagements together. And in our private life it was obviously turbulent."*

Separation, if not divorce, was on the cards, and it was almost incidental that the Duke of York's marriage was heading for disaster, too. With the divorce from Mark Phillips by Princess Anne, the three married Windsor children were in a terrible mess.

All the Windsor family values, as encouraged so much by Queen Victoria, were in a shambles. But the only one that really mattered was the marriage of the Wales-ses. And that was about to be hit by the publication of Andrew Morton's bombshell book *Diana: Her True Story*.

Left: While Diana struggled to maintain a composed public face, inside her emotions were in turmoil. Here she is seen during the ceremony of Trooping the Colour in 1992.

Below: The pensive look is suggestive of inner troubles. One of the penalties of fame is that private anguish cannot be kept from the public eye.

Above: Cruising in the sun on King Juan Carlos' yacht Fortuna *off Palma, Majorca in 1986, but the atmosphere between Charles and Diana was frosty.*

Written with her tacit consent, it portrayed a lonely, neurotic princess, driven to tears, bulimia and tantrums by her unhappy marriage. It exposed the prince as a distant father, uncaring husband and adulterer.

The book disclosed that, even as the fairy-tale couple had honeymooned on the royal yacht *Britannia*, the prince was in regular touch with his long-time companion and mistress, Mrs Parker Bowles.

Doubts about the origin of the Morton revelations were quashed when, three days after the first extract of the book was published, the princess paid a visit to her friend Carolyn Bartholomew, who had furnished much telling material for the book.

Above: A mother's love – Diana's joy on being reunited with Wills and Harry during a tour of Canada in 1991 is plain to see.

Diana thought the book might help: 'I was at the end of my tether', she said. 'I was desperate. I think I was so fed up with being seen as someone who was a basket case, because I am a very strong person and I know that causes complications in the system I live in.'

Above: In sombre mood after Charles' skiing companions had been killed in an accident in Klosters in 1988.
Right: Diana in tears shortly after the publication of Andrew Morton's book.

After the book, though, 'maybe people have a better understanding. Maybe there's a lot of women out there who suffer on the same level, but in a different environment, who are unable to stand up for themselves because their self-esteem is cut in two.'

The Morton book, she agreed, had been devastating: 'I think the royal family were shocked and horrified and very disappointed. What had been hidden, or rather what we thought had been hidden, then came out in the open and was spoken about on a daily basis, and the pressure was for us to sort ourselves out in some way.

'Were we going to stay together, or were we going to separate? And the word separation and divorce kept coming up in the media on a daily basis. We struggled along. We did our engagements together. And in our private life it was obviously turbulent.'

The princess continued to maintain her extraordinary hold on public sympathy and affection despite the publication of tapes of intimate telephone conversations, known as the 'Squidgy Affair', apparently between her and James Gilbey, whose voice could be heard professing love.

And that disastrous tour of Korea by the ill-at-ease Prince and Princess in November 1992 sealed the fate of the marriage. It was plain to all that the marriage of the royal Glums was all but over.

In fact talks about their future were going on behind the scenes. Press speculation of a split was never-ending. And Diana was telling a woman friend in a private conversation (which later was said to have been bugged by MI5): 'I've been acting the biggest role of

my career for 10 years. I should be in movies. I'm going. So are the boys. It's an impossible situation.'

But she denied rumours that she was demanding her own palace: 'All I want is Charles to leave Kensington Palace', she said. 'We could see what the public were requiring. They wanted clarity in a situation that was obviously becoming intolerable.

'So we got the lawyers together, we discussed separation. Obviously there were a lot of people to discuss it with – the Prime Minister, Her Majesty – and then it moved itself, so to speak.'

By December they had agreed to a legal separation and it was announced by Buckingham Palace and in the House of Commons by Prime Minister John Major, who said there were no plans for a divorce.

For Diana it brought 'deep, deep, profound sadness. Because we had struggled to

Above and right: The official tour of Korea in November 1992 marked the low-water mark of the marriage. The estrangement of the couple was all too clear to see; on account of their miserable demeanour, the Wales were nicknamed the Glums by the press travelling with them on this tour.

Above: A poignant scene – the last family Christmas card, dating from 1991. The photograph was taken by Lord Snowdon.

keep it going, but obviously we'd both run out of steam. And in a way I suppose it could have been a relief for us both that we'd finally made our minds up.

'But my husband asked for the separation and I supported it. I came from a divorced background and I didn't want to go into that one again.'

Of the children, she said: 'I asked my husband if we could put the announcement out before they came back from school for Christmas holidays, because they were protected in the school they were at. I went down a week beforehand and explained what was happening.

'And they took it as children do – asking lots of questions – and I hoped I was able to reassure them. But who knows?

'I think the announcement had a huge effect on me and Charles, and the children were very much out of it, in the sense that they were tucked away at school.

'I take some responsibility that our marriage went the way it did. I'll take half of it, but I won't take any more than that, because it takes two to get in this situation. We both made mistakes.'

News of the royal split was announced as Diana was working. 'I was on an engagement up North', she remembered. 'I heard it on the radio, and it was just very, very sad. Really sad. The fairytale had come to an end.'

Above and right: On the tour of India in February 1992 signs of open hostility between the couple became obvious to see. Princess Diana turned her head away when Charles made to kiss her. And in a move that must have been calculated to engage public sympathy, Diana posed alone and forlorn in front of the Taj Mahal, the most spectacular monument to marital love and fidelity in the world.

Above: The final homecoming – Diana's hearse at the entrance to Althorp and its floral tribute.

Goodbye England's rose,
From a country lost without your soul,
Who'll miss the wings of your compassion,
More than you'll ever know.

As it all ended, the cortege was carried out and halted at the west end of the Abbey for a minute's silence, observed nationwide.

The half-muffled bells of the Abbey rang out their dirge, and Diana left on her long last journey, by hearse, through streets lined with more people, more flowers, back home to her family's Althorp estate in Northamptonshire.

All along the 77-mile route crowds hurled bouquets and single blooms at the hearse, like some grim battle of the flowers, and cried out their goodbyes until she arrived at Althorp.

There, at a short private service attended by the Spencer family, Prince Charles and her sons, they finally laid Diana to rest, wearing a formal, long-sleeved black dress she bought a few weeks earlier and had never worn, and with a rosary given to her by Mother Teresa of Calcutta.

Her simple grave is on a beautiful, tree-filled and newly-consecrated island on an ornamental lake called The Oval – a place Diana loved since she was a girl and where she and her sisters and sons had planted oaks for future generations to see and enjoy.

It was chosen rather than the traditional Spencer burial place – the family chapel in the parish church of St Mary the Virgin – so that sightseers would be deterred from laying constant siege to the quiet village of Great Brington.

And so, as Earl Spencer said, 'the grave can be properly looked after by the family and visited in privacy by her sons'.

'A wonderful place', said former Spencer housekeeper Betty Andrew, now 76. 'I used to go there in the early mornings to gather greenery to go with all the flowers in the house. It's beautiful and quiet and peaceful. A perfect place for Diana.'

By the evening of that achingly sad day she was at rest there, away from the spotlights and the headlines, the flashguns and the limelight in which she'd lived most of her cruelly short life.

Away from the rumours, the smears, the lies. Away from the agonies and anxieties that had plagued her.

She lies there now, alone on her own isolated and tranquil island, where no cares or concerns can reach her, where nothing and no-one can touch her.

The people's princess is the sleeping princess. In peace. At last.

Above: Diana's final resting place at Althorp – an island, away from the prying lenses of the Press.

Epitaph

"My sister – the unique, the complex, the extraordinary and irreplaceable Diana..."

"Diana was the very essence of compassion, of duty, of style, of beauty. All over the world, she was a symbol of selfless humanity. All over the world, a standard-bearer for the rights of the truly downtrodden, a very British girl who transcended nationality. Someone with a natural nobility who was classless and who proved in the last year that she needed no royal title to continue to generate her particular brand of magic."

Earl Spencer, from his funeral address,
Westminster Abbey, London, September 6th, 1997

Picture credits

The publishers would like to thank the following for their help in providing photographs for this book.

Alpha, London: 12-13, 14 top left and bottom right, 15, 17 bottom right, 18 bottom left, 19 top left and bottom, 32 bottom, top right, 37 top right, 38 inset top left, 40 top left, 41 top left and top right, 43 upper and lower right, 44 top, 45 bottom left, 47 top left, 49 top and bottom, 66, 67 top left and bottom left, 72-73, 75, 78 bottom right, 82 bottom left and right, 86 bottom left, 87, 88 top centre and bottom left, 90 right, 95 middle (Dave Chancellor), 101 bottom right,114 top right, 116 top left; **BBC:** 60-61 top centre; **Dave Benett:** 95 bottom right; **Camera Press:** 14 top right, 24, 28-9 (Lichfield), 30 bottom left, 35 (Lichfield), 55 (Snowdon), 68 top and bottom left, 76 top left, 84 all pictures, 85 all pictures, 90 bottom left, 92 top right, 95 bottom left, 101 left, 102, 139 (Patrick Demarchelier); **Eastern Counties Newspapers:** 18 top; **Fox/Central Press:** 22 top, 23;**The Independent:** 132 bottom (Brian Harris); **Julian Herbert:** 43 lower left; **Mirror Group Newspapers:** 6, 7 (Kent Gavin),17 left and top right, 18 bottom right and inset bottom centre, 20 bottom right, 21 left, 25 top left, centre left and bottom left, 27, 31 top, 32 top right, 33, 34 top, centre and bottom, 37 bottom, 38 top right and bottom, 39, 42 bottom centre, 43 top left, 45 right, 47 top right, bottom left and bottom right, 48 (Kent Gavin), 50, 51, 52 (Kent Gavin), 53, 54 (left), 54 right (Kent Gavin), 56, 58-59 (Kent Gavin), 60 inset top left, 61 right, 62, 63, 64 top, centre and bottom, 67 right, 72 inset, 74 inset top left and top right, 77, 78 top left (Kent Gavin) bottom left (Kent Gavin), 79 (Kent Gavin), 80, 81, 83, 86 inset top left (Kent Gavin), 89 (Kent Gavin), 91 (Kent Gavin), 92 bottom (Kent Gavin), 93, 94 (Kent Gavin), 96 inset top left and right, 97, 98-100 all pictures (Kent Gavin), 103-109 (Kent Gavin), 114 inset top left and bottom, 115 top left and bottom left, 121 inset, 124-125; **Portman Press:** 20 bottom left; **Press Association:** 12 inset top left,16, 19 top right, 20 centre right, 110-111, 115 top right and inset bottom right, 116 bottom left, 117 left, 118 top left and bottom left, 119 top right and middle and bottom left, 120; **Press Association Rota Photographers:** 128-131, 132 top pictures, 133-137; **Rex Features:** 5, 20 top left and top right, 21 right, 22 bottom, 25 right, 26 left and right, 30-31 centre bottom, 37 top left, 42 top and bottom right, 46 top right, 57, 58 inset, 60 bottom, 61 left, 68 bottom right, 69 top, 74 right, 76 right, 117 top right (Peter Heimsath) and bottom right, 118-119 top, 122 right, 123 top; **Reuters:** 116 right, 118 bottom right, 119 botom right; **Solent News Agency:** 36; **Syndication International:** 28 inset, 30 top, 32 top left, 40 top right (Kent Gavin), 40 bottom, 41 bottom, 44 bottom, 45 top left; **Universal Pictures International:** 71; Steve Wood: 95 top middle

Every effort has been made to contact copyright holders in cases where ownership is not clear.

Princess Diana's Charities

United Kingdom

The Diana, Princess of Wales Memorial Fund
Kensington Palace
London W8 4PU

The British Red Cross*
Anti-Personnel Land Mines Campaign
No 9 Grosvenor Crescent
London SW1X 7EJ
**Ceased to be official patron in 1996*

Centrepoint Soho
Bewlay House
2 Swallow Place
London W1R 7AA

English National Ballet
Markova House
39 Jay Mews
London SW7 2EF

The Leprosy Mission
Goldhay Way
Orton Goldhay
Peterborough PE2 5GZ

National Aids Trust
Princess Diana Fund
New City Cloisters
188-196 Old Street
London EC1V 9FR

Royal Marsden NHS Trust
Fulham Rd
London SW3 6JJ

Great Ormond St Hospital for Children NHS Trust
Great Ormond St
London WC1N 3JH

United States

American Red Cross
17th and D Streets NW
Washington, D.C. 20006